Stories of a
Speech Pathologist

Stories of a Speech Pathologist

Volume 1.0

BRIAN HURLEY

ISBN: 1979853746
ISBN 13: 9781979853743

Authors Note: This collection of stories initially was an outlet to deal with the stresses of the job, and to maintain focus. After many encounters, and time spent with these special individuals I decided to compile this collection of stories. With these patients in mind a percentage of every book sold will be donated to Alzheimer's/Dementia research. If you enjoyed, laughed, or learned from this book please share with your friends and family. Thank you and I truly hope you enjoy!

Special thanks to Illustrator, Guest Editors, and Friends:

Jackie Briggs, Illustrator
Ariel Price, Editor
Sarah and Sean Clayton, Editors

Social Media:

Instagram @storiesofaspeechpath
Write a Review and Track What's New:
Storiesofaspeechpath.com

Table of Contents

In My Sleeve

Entry 1

TODAY IT'S IN MY SLEEVE, TOMORROW IT'S...

I enter the room to work with this sweet lady who is blind and very hard of hearing. As we are practicing her oral motor exercises, I notice there is something wrong with the patient's arm, more specifically her elbow. Her elbow appears to be dislodged or severely swollen right where her sleeve meets her arm. I ask her if she is in pain, but because of her cognitive status she couldn't provide a straight answer. I lift her sleeve expecting to see some sort of injury or brace, only to find a breast staring me in the face (awkward turtle). Apparently 90+ years of gravity results in the ability to get your boob caught in your sleeve, and flipped around your arm, trying to escape from your shirt. Thus, the elbow that had a nipple was born.

Entry 2

FLASHER

As I started my therapeutic meal with a patient I draped a towel over her lap to catch the pending food that is about to amass on her lap. The session is going well as I see some positive improvements and decreased signs and symptoms of penetration/aspiration. I'm wrapping up and remove the towel the patient looks down and asks, "What's all this?" referring to the sheet draped over her lap. I asked her if she would like to remove the sheet, the patient responds, "Yes." As I begin to remove the sheet I quickly realize she has on no under garments. I point this out to the patient and tell her we are going to leave the sheet on until an aide can come and dress her. The patient is confused, so I clarify that she has no draws on. The patient says, "I do have draws on" and proceeds to lift the sheet, only to realize she indeed does not have any on, places the sheet back over her lap. She then giggles and says, "Want to see?" again lifting the sheet anyways and giggling creepily. "Really, lady, I don't want to see," I think to myself, as I drape the sheet back over her lap.

Entry 3

FLASHER FOLLOW-UP

Follow-up: I'm in the middle of a session working with a patient who is in the later stages of dementia, and claims to be uncomfortable with complaints of soreness on her bottom from sitting in a wheelchair. The patient now known as "flasher" (who is no longer on my caseload) is wheeled into the room and greets me with a big hello. Flasher takes note of the discomfort of my current patient and starts to console her and tell her she knows what she is going through. Meanwhile, I stop the session to attempt to find a cushion to resolve the discomfort. While a nurse is assisting me in looking for a cushion, the patient is confused and remains in discomfort. I assure her that a nurse is looking for a cushion and point out, for reference, the cushion flasher is sitting on.

As I am describing the cushion to the patient that she will be receiving a large, soft, nice…… flasher yells out "COCK!" she chuckles to herself and states, "I couldn't resist." Someone has certainly made the best of her situation and clearly gives minimal fucks.

Entry 4

ANOMIA... BUT REALLY WHAT DID YOU JUST SAY

- **Anomia:** part of anomia is the loss or difficulty with the ability to name common objects.

Patient comes in to the therapy room and sees her reflection in the tinted window. She states, "It looks like a torn penis went through my hair!" Not sure what the hell that's supposed to mean, or if it was some phrase that I had never heard, so I ask her what she just said. The patient realizes the mistake and laughs about it, then says, "Uh uh uh uh tornado!" Classic! Watch out for the torn penis look.

Entry 5

Reality of the Job and Helping Everyone

In the middle of a session, a patient whispers to me, "Forever and always," to which I respond, "What?" The patient clarifies, "Forever and always I'll hate niggers." Not a fan of bigotry, I make a face and try to continue on with the session. The patient starts to explain herself, to which I had no option but to say, "You don't have to explain yourself, let's continue with these exercises and finish up." Sometimes you just have to grit your teeth and power through the harsh reality that people will constantly surprise you in good and bad ways.

Rumble From Down Under

Entry 6

WHOEVER SAID GIRL'S FARTS SMELL LIKE ROSES WAS WRONG

A cognitively intact patient during a dysphagia management session rips ass, (it's not a dainty small poof, but rather a "that's how my father would have let it rip on the couch watching football" kind of fart). She then coughs to try to cover it up. Not wanting to offend her, I try to keep my shit eating grin from appearing on my face. Not ten minutes later, she rips ass again as loud and proud as the first time, only this time she states, "Ah that feels better." Home girl, we ain't close like that, I don't want to sit in your stank filled room... your farts don't smell like roses. I proceed to wrap up the session and evacuate. I was just glad that first fart was not "a gamble and lose" situation, because I'm not sure I could have handled that heat.

Entry 7

CALL ME "LIEUT"

A new friend on my caseload at the skilled nursing facility tells me to call him "Lieut," as in Lieutenant. One day during a therapeutic meal in the dining room, which is set up in a white tablecloth swanky fashion, he counts around the room (thankfully not in Japanese) and sees that there are only 4 male patients, the rest are proper ladies attending lunch. After this realization, he jumps into asking me if I had ever heard of "SHIT ON A BRICK" (yelling because he is really hard of hearing and does not believe hearing aids help, so he assumes the rest of us can't hear either). Thinking to myself, I have heard of shitting a brick, but never shit on a brick... He explains to me that "shit on a brick" is a meal prepared in the military made of ground beef and gravy poured over a hard ass biscuit. After sufficiently getting at least the ladies in the room who can hear to look over and gawk, I think to myself, "At least he is not talking about his days in Japan." The day prior, he started counting in Japanese, so naturally I ask him how he learned. He tells me he was in Japan then laughs out loud to himself. Nonchalantly states, "We killed them" = NO FILTER (not the cutesy I took a picture with no Instagram kind of filter).

Entry 8

Positive outlook

Upon doing an evaluation for speech and language with a patient with Parkinson's, it becomes immediately apparent that he like many patients with Parkinson's, has a poor perception of vocal loudness which is interfering with communication effectiveness. When talking with the patient about therapy and working on increasing vocal volume the patient gives the best response I have heard yet….. "Why the Hell would I want to do that? The ladies have to lean in close to hear me." Touché, valid point sir! Hahaha to have such an optimistic look at a paramount struggle to be understood is just classic. The same patient when asked hobbies/interests his first response was sports (as he is a sports enthusiast), his second response was with minimum volume. Asked to repeat himself with increased volume the patient yells "SEX". One. Track. Mind.

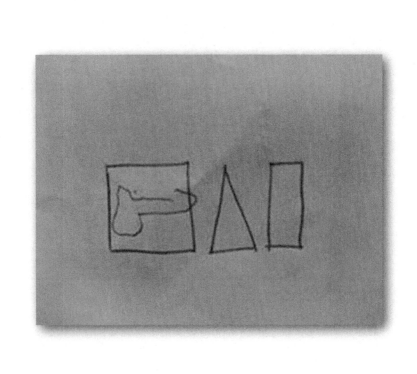

Entry 9

SUBCONSCIOUS SEX

This gem of a story comes from my co-worker (photo, actual photo from evaluation). My co-worker was administering the St. Louis University Mental Status Examination and we came to the section where you prompt the patient to place an "X" in the triangle. This patient goes to work and comes up with the following....

Apparently he heard or was thinking place a penis in the square. Once he was asked to take a closer look at what was drawn, the patient cracks up and has a moment of insight to what he had just crafted. "Isn't that the strangest thing" the patient replies, "That's not an X, or the triangle." HAHA have to give credit where credit is due, a penis in the box he must have been watching Saturday Night Live (dick in a box reference).

Entry 10

LOAF OF BREAD, BOTTLE OF WINE

While covering my co-workers caseload I pick up her patient from the lock down dementia unit, and ask how his day is going. His response, "Loaf of bread, bottle of wine," everyone in the rehab department knows this gentleman and his catch phrase. Must say "loaf of bread, bottle of wine," is not a bad day I suppose. We get into the therapy room and he proceeds to make himself comfortable, kicks his leg over the arm of the wheelchair and gives me a, "Come on, let's get on with it". Ah, what the heck, you're comfortable and want to work like that I'll roll with it. We had a good session and it's time to bring him back… "Ok sir, can you place your leg in front of you," I say to him. The patient gives me a death stare, and with a few more cues, and taps to his leg he refuses, and says "I'm fine just take me back." "O.K." not the typical response I would give, nor suggest. Concerned about him catching his pant leg, I proceed slowly. Rolling down the hall straight ahead is the row of ladies who typically can be found sitting in front of the nurse's station (most of which contently staring off into the distance). A lady is looking right at my patient, as we get closer to the hall we need to turn down the patient feels the need to yell, "WHAT?! IT'S A BIG COCK!" to the lady staring at his lounging posture... ok, and we are turning..... Not a care in the world! "loaf of bread, bottle of wine" a real Casanova haha.

Banana Shopping

Entry 11

BANANA JOKE

During a typical meal trying to upgrade a patient's diet I find myself running back and forth from the kitchen to the private dining area for patients with dysphagia. Upon my third trip to the kitchen to find some mechanical soft consistency that the patient will tolerate and actually eat, I come back with a banana. The patient does well and her ability to masticate has drastically improved over the week, but that's not really what this story is about. I go to treat a patient that also has meals in this private dining area later in the day and he approaches asking, "Can I share a joke with you?" I have quickly learned over the past year whenever a patient says anything along these lines the answer is always yes. Stop what you're doing and listen. The patient goes, "Seeing you bring that lady a banana earlier reminded me of a joke I know." Proceed… "O.k. there are two old maids who walk in to a grocery store to buy some bananas. They notice the bananas are on sale 3 for a dollar. The one old maid says to the other what are we gonna do? The other old maid replies… we will just eat the third one." UH-MAZE-ING! I don't care who you are that shit is funny.

Entry 12

FOREPLAY

A 94 year old prisoner of war with pretty intact cognition is in the middle of a therapy session working on functional descriptions. A fun little way to work on using language to maximize the message with limited semantics. He grabs the next slip of paper out of a bucket with words on it, and the objective is to give a good enough description in a few words to have the other person guess what word is on the chosen slip of paper. He gives me the first hint, "Foreplay"... I give him a puzzled look and say, "C'mon man that is only one word, and not very descriptive." He seems confident in his choice of words and expands by saying, "It is a part of foreplay if your running around with someone." I respond with, "A kiss?" To which he responds, "Close." "A hug?" He says, "No far from it"… still very puzzled I ask him to provide better detail. He says, "It gets everywhere." O.K. hmmm. So of course I guess whip cream. He gets a laugh and says, "no." "Chocolate?" "No." So I ask, "do guys and girls have it?" He says, "no," my next guess is, "lipstick." "YES that's it! It gets everywhere in foreplay. I know that when the lipstick goes on that's the sign." Hahahaha that's great…. The next slip he gets he starts off by saying, "Ok this one too has to do with foreplay." Really man, I know what is on these slips there is not some bucket full of slips dealing with foreplay. He goes, "its itchy." What The Hell? I'm gonna need a better description than that to start guessing. He says, "Yea if you're running through the bush chasing a girl you might get it on you and it's itchy." I guess, "Poison ivy?" "Yes!"

Entry 13

ERECTION

A woman with an impressive background and education recently suffered a stroke mostly manifesting itself in the form of expressive communication difficulties, more specifically expressive aphasia with anomia. Working on some confrontational naming and semantic mapping techniques I present a photo of an Egyptian structure. The patient immediately says with certainty, "ERECTION!," realizes the error made laughs hysterically for a few minutes then says, "Egyptian," shaking her head still laughing. Oh how the human brain works, and the little things that could otherwise be extremely embarrassing or frustrating can also be funny, and bring a smile to your face in the midst of regaining the ability to communicate.

Entry 14

CONSUMMATING A RELATIONSHIP

A patient of mine, who is a little on the flirty side with all the women in the facility whom work there lets me know that one lucky lady and him consummated their relationship. Now I have seen my fair share of inappropriate interactions between staff and patients that exhibit flirty conduct such as sticking their rear out and letting a patient slap it which is degrading for both parties in my opinion. I was not sure what this fellow meant, but he was as serious as he could be. He then smiles and said, "Yup, she wiped my ass, and in here that's good enough as consummating my relationship with her," then laughed out loud. That's fantastic, a situation that could be embarrassing and tough made into a pretty comical outlook!

Entry 15

BODY FUNCTIONS

This next story is about explaining to a patient who refuses to believe there is a problem with his swallowing, that there is one. I explain to the patient for the 20th or so time with visuals and written descriptions what is occurring with their swallowing mechanism. I tell him that food/liquid is entering his lungs. The response: "if it doesn't go in your stomach, and goes in your lungs how does it digest?" I think we are making progress on the retention with max cueing and visuals.

Entry 16

Going the extra mile

My department, over 90% female, is always having potlucks and events for any occasion. A male patient of mine asks me during therapy about an upcoming potluck and goes, "It's a big deal to these girls, you can bring water!" Haha my water will stack up nicely to the extravagant meals prepared by the rest of the department.

Entry 17

DENTURE TEST

A patient of mine I have been working with for a while, I always have to ask her to put her dentures in for meals, once again does not have her dentures in place. Each time I ask her to repeat a phrase to ensure a good fit, and to make sure no floating of the dentures is occurring. On this day, now familiar with the routine, goes, "Want me to say a nursery rhyme?" Not sure what I would get in response of course I say, "Yes!" "Mary had a little lamb, and its fleece was white as snow, then her father shot it dead, now she brings the lamb to school, between two slices of bread!" WOW just wow haha. The patient then asks me if I would like to hear another one, of course I would! "3 blind mice, see how they run, the farmer's wife cut off their tails with a carving knife!" WOW! Never failed to be amazed at what some people say. They may not rhyme perfectly but definitely got my attention.

Entry 18

WOULD YOU ASK WILLIE NELSON FOR DIRECTIONS?

This one comes from my clinical days but a classic none the less. I walk in to perform a cognitive evaluation on a middle aged woman who happens to resemble the likes of Willie Nelson. Double braided gray hair, with altered mental status. This lady is what people might say "out to lunch" not oriented to time, person, situation, reality or…. Earth. In any case, I continue with my evaluation and ask her, "If you were lost and didn't know where you were, and needed help what would you do?" The patient responded with, "Well….. I would crawl up daddy's back (long pause) turn my head to the left (long pause) and…. Sniff (actions provided by patient)"…. Not sure where that's gonna get ya but hey, goes to show dad knows best! Two weeks later we follow-up with this patient and she recalls this particular day for us. She made slow and steady progress back to joining us in reality, and being oriented, and eventually back to her baseline cognitive status. She tells us she recalls us asking her these evaluation questions, responding, and knowing that she wasn't giving good reasonable answers. She described it as an out of body experience. A little further information for those wondering, her toxicology reports were negative, she was not "off her meds," no prior psychosis events, and all vitals within normal limits. Cue extraterrestrial music now.......

Entry 19

Not me no mo

I walk in to do a bedside swallow evaluation with a patient who is blind (please no elbow brace), and attempt to complete a swallow evaluation. A little background information on this patient and how she found herself in the hospital. This was no ordinary visit, as this patient was in the care of someone around the clock at home and this caregiver could no longer take on the responsibility. The caregiver decided to bring her to the patient's primary care provider. The decision to bring her to the doctor's office was not for a check-up but rather a drop off. Once faced with the predicament of a patient that now has become homeless secondary to a caregiver who could no longer take on that responsibility, the doctor sent the patient to the hospital so they could find placement for the patient in a home/facility where she could be cared for. This patient is pleasant and decides to inform me of how she found out she had a hematoma previously. welllllllll....

Patient: "So I was at this place and there was a brown recluse spider, you know the dangerous kind. I flipped out when it was on my arm, I threw my jacket down, and requested to be sent to the hospital... you know this was before I was blind."

Me: "o.k. go on"

Patient: "Well, I ended up going hospital and they found a hematoma in my brain"

Me: "Ah well that's good they found it"

Patient: "Yea but I had taken a line of crystal"......... (long pause)

Me: "Ok what do you mean?"

Patient: "I took a line of crystal and was freaking out. That's why I was brought to the hospital and they found the hematoma. That was when I could see"

Me: "Ah, well at least they found it!"

Patient: "Yea, and now people ask me why I'm so happy. I tell them I have lived and done the things I want to, so I am happy, I don't care that I can't see."

Say no to crystal meth kids!

Entry 20

EAT YOUR VEGGIES

I return to an old contract location and get a new clientele. Amongst this population is a sweet lady with pretty moderately advanced dementia. One of the goals for this patient is for generative naming and to increased functional communication. I start presenting a naming task for generative naming and utilize the category "vegetables". The patient gets 2-3 then I start cueing by adding, "How about vegetables colored red." The patient responds, "Radish, beets..." to which I make a very visible face of disgust. She realizes this and questions why I'm making this face. I explain to her, "I despise beets, and think they taste like dirt!!" She calmly and full of confusion and disbelief states, "WELL I think they are great, I DON'T KNOW WHAT DIRT TASTES LIKE". Hahaha you got me there, I stopped, and had to think how literal, and touché yes, to say it tastes like dirt would imply I know how dirt tastes. She then asks me to save the next thing that I have that tastes like dirt so she can try it.

Entry 21

MY ACHY BREAKY... WHAT!

Picking up a new caseload from a previous therapists has its struggles. One of those struggles is you walk-in on day one and have a caseload of 10 patients, give or take, and there is no way you can do thorough reviews on all your patients history prior to meeting them. One of my new lovely patients is on caseload for cognitive thera-py post hospitalization. This is a high level cognitive pa-tient who is on caseload more or less to make sure she is safe to return to her previous living environment which is home independent. Of course she has PT and OT work-ing with her for strength and mobility purposes, however I'm tasked with assessing and treating cognitive aspects to assure a safe transition home. This patient is in a wide wheelchair and I'm wheeling her into my office as she

states, "Please don't hit the wall it's very painful." Ok....
I mean sometimes I take my patients for a wild fast ride
down the halls, but that's by request ONLY, and I don't
want to get my wheelchair driver's license revoked. So,
don't worry I will try my best not to hit walls. I continue to
get to know her and ask what has happened, she tells me
she hurts. So of course I ask where, to which she replies,
"All over". Ok let's be real, all over is a lot of real estate,
can you please narrow it down for me. She then states,
"I hurt from my breasts to my vagina". Whoaaaa, ok now
I'm perplexed. "So you boke your sternum?" No, "I broke
multiple vertebrae". Well indeed then yes I see how you
may hurt from point A to B.... I'm beginning to think "I
hurt all over" is appropriate.

Entry 22

REAL TALK

Few stories here have outlined the struggles and hardships we as therapists face, and I feel it's necessary to share those as well. One of the, if not the toughest part of my job, involves patients who are struggling with dysphagia. Part of our evaluation, care, and treatment/management includes diet recommendations. I pray for the days I have a patient that is on the cusp of success/failure (yes failure for those in the speech world who despise the use of pass/fail during instrumental evaluation), and walks away succeeding. This might not mean a whole lot to many reading this, so let me explain. A patient who is complicated or elderly with a terminal illness or progressive neurological condition who suffers from swallowing complications may face a time where a decision to have an altered diet or feeding tube falls upon them. Eating is something that they (all of us) typically take for granted, this can be the thing that eventually causes death from recurrent aspiration pneumonias (material entering the airway/lungs causing infection, or respiratory failure as a result). So yes, failure I believe is the appropriate word or at least how a patient perceives the outcome of a poor prognosis with swallow etiology from a modified barium swallow study (a study we perform with radiologists utilizing barium contrast mixed with foods and liquids to objectively assess a person's swallow with video x-ray). These are the patients that when young, healthy, and could benefit from a feeding tube have positive outlooks, however those that are complex or elderly don't have the same prognosis. The patients that are not good candidates are the ones we have to explain to, or the families, that there is a "safer" way to maintain hydration/nutrition, however the patient will most likely continue to aspirate on their own secretions or potentially from reflux. This is when hospice/palliative care consults become a part of our profession (when a feeding tube is not a viable option, and the patient has dysphagia with other complexities that present a poor prognosis). Sometimes patients and/or families have planned out their wishes to continue to eat by mouth despite high known risks of aspiration which is slightly easier to deal with, but never a fun conversation none the less. Each day I apply skills and knowledge with plans to improve one's impairments, sometimes this just is not possible, knowing the difference is important. This entry hopefully inspires some to plan their future (that means putting it in writing).

Entry 23

STALKER WITH A WALKER

While endearing and flattering, you don't always want to be asked to dinner or to take your shirt off. I have a new patient that has suffered 2 strokes, we will call her Suzan (not actual name). Suzan is a pleasant lady that was difficult to work with at first, but eventually started to enjoy working with me, maybe a bit too much. She began a streak of non-compliance with other therapies where she would only work with me which is counterproductive for physical and occupational therapies. One day we are in the middle of a therapy session as she would commonly say, "Well, I need to go I have things I need to do." Being the therapist I am, I of course say, "Well, what are these things, and are they something I can help with?" Since this was a ploy to leave early she had no response and continued with the session. Five minutes later she states, "Well….. " (at this point I'm assuming she is going to give the routine response of "I have things I need to go do"). Not today, instead she goes, "Well... since this has been going so well, you and I working together, I'd be delighted to take you to dinner!" Of course I decline, a sweet offer but clearly not happening.

Fast forward to the next session: I'm in my office in the midst of a session and she goes, "Can you take your shirt off?" (with a smirk)

Me: "Excuse me what?"

Suzan: "It's wrinkled, I'll iron it for you."

Me: "Ohhhhh well thank you, but I can take care of that, but really thank you for the offer."

Fast Fast forward: Working on an exercise where the language portion requires listing things within a certain category. I present a category of "things you do in the winter"… With this exercise there are letters for the initial letter of a word for the patient to utilize in order to name things that you "do in the winter"… I knew this would be a relatively difficult exercise for the patient and she started off with two quick accurate responses:

Suzan: "Ski"

Suzan: "Snowball fight"

Shit, she's on a roll. Maybe not as difficult as I thought it would be for her. Then... she's stuck on the next one. So I repeat the instructions, "Provide something you do in the winter that starts with the letter S"

She then replies with, "Suzan!" and laughs I said, "Something you do in the winter," she replies, "Yes, I know Suzan!"... **Gag**

The rest of the week I had some strange encounters with this patient starting with returning to my office and seeing the occupational therapist working with her in my office because she refused to work with anyone outside of that space. Then on two occasions she wrote a note and left it stating, "I stopped by and no one was home, sorry I missed you."

I finish a session and I'm walking her back to her wing of the nursing facility, then ask her, "Where she would like to go (dining area, t.v. room etc...)." She looks at me confused and goes, "Well where are you going? I thought we had two hours." I explain to her we had 45 minutes and now I need to work with other patients. She then responds with, "Well I'm gonna take you to my room, and sit you down on my bed" WHAT! Ok you are TOO much, I kindly ask a nurse's assistant to assist diffuse this situation and take over.

Things have escalated and now she just wanders into the therapy department at all hours of the day looking for me... I find myself on a random Thursday, camped out peeking through a closet door as my co-workers have to tell her they have not seen me. Is this what it has come to? I have to hide from my patients? Oh this job never fails to surprise me!

Made in the USA
Middletown, DE
26 January 2019